513 4

Measuring

David Kirkby

First published in Great Britain by Heinemann Library
an imprint of Heinemann Publishers (Oxford) Ltd
Halley Court, Jordan Hill, Oxford OX2 8EJ

MADRID ATHENS PARIS
FLORENCE PRAGUE WARSAW
PORTSMOUTH NH CHICAGO SAO PAULO
SINGAPORE TOKYO MELBOURNE AUCKLAND
IBADAN GABERONE JOHANNESBURG

Designed by The Pinpoint Design Company
Printed in China

99 98 97 96 95
10 9 8 7 6 5 4 3 2 1

ISBN 0431 07958 7

British Library Cataloguing in Publication Data available on
request from the British Library.

Acknowledgements
The Publishers would like to thank the following
for the kind loan of equipment and materials
used in this book: Boswells, Oxford; The Early Learning
Centre; Lewis', Oxford; W. H. Smith; N. E. S. Arnold.
Special thanks to the children of St Francis C.E. First School

Photography: Chris Honeywell, Oxford

Cover photograph: Chris Honeywell, Oxford

contents contents

tallest

shortest

This doll is tallest.

This doll
is shortest.

4

Which is tallest?

1   2   3   4

To do:
Copy the towers above.
Now draw some more
bricks on number 1
to make it the tallest.

longest

shortest

This is shortest.

This is longest.

6

Which is longest?
Which is shortest?

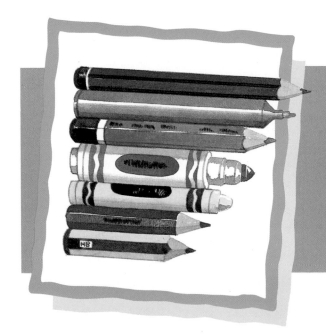

To do:
Find some pens and
pencils. Line them up.
Put the longest at the
top. Put the shortest at
the bottom.

Sometimes you need to know how long or how tall something is.

You can measure with anything.

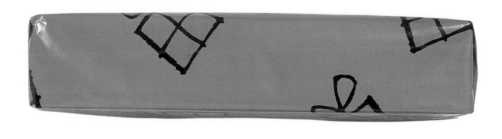

Measure with the same thing.
This present is 9 pasta tubes long.

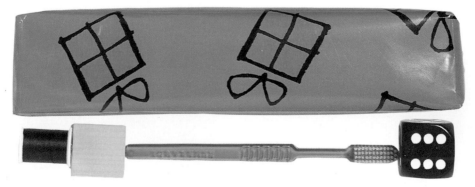

It is hard to measure well with different things.

8

How many boxes tall?

To do:
Use your open hand to measure with.
How many hands long is your table?
How many hands tall is your table?

It is best if everyone uses the same thing to measure.
We measure in centimetres (cm for short) and metres (m for short).
100 centimetres = 1 metre.

Kieran is 132 cm tall.

He is 59 cm around.

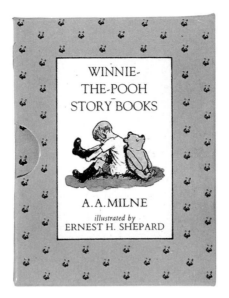

How many
cm long?

How many cm wide?

To do:
Estimate (guess) how many cm long your foot is.
Measure it.
Estimate (guess) how many cm it is around your head.
Measure it.

We use scales to
weigh things.
They tell us
which is heaviest.
The heaviest thing
makes the scales go down.

The dinosaur is heavier.
The ball is lighter.

What is lighter?

To do:
What is lighter
than a bed?
What is heavier
than a ball?

13

We weigh things in grams (g for short) and kilograms (kg for short). 1000 grams = 1 kilogram.

These sweets weigh 1 kilogram.

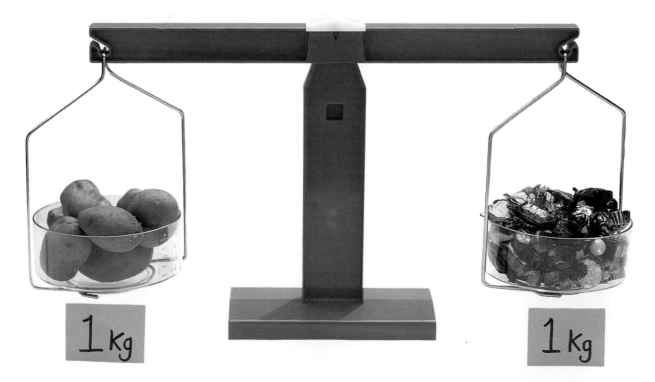

1 kg

1 kg

These potatoes weigh 1 kilogram.

14

How much does this flour weigh?

To do:
Does the packet of biscuits weigh more than the bag of sugar?

The jug holds more juice than the glass. We say that the capacity of the jug is greater than the capacity of the glass.

6 glasses of juice will fill this jug. The capacity is the amount of juice the jug will hold.

We measure liquid capacity in
millilitres (ml for short) and
litres (l for short).

To do:
Estimate (guess) which
will hold the most
water: a cup or a bowl.

Fill a cup and bowl
with water to see
if you were right.

Clocks measure time in minutes and hours.
The long hand points to the 12 (to show o'clock).

The short hand points to the 8 (to show the hour).

This clock shows 8 o'clock.

One clock shows a different time
from all the others.
What time does it show?
What time do the other clocks show?

To do:
What time is it?

19

Digital clocks do not have hands. They show the time just using numbers. This clock shows 8 o'clock. The number before : shows the hour. The number after : shows the minutes. **:00** shows o'clock.

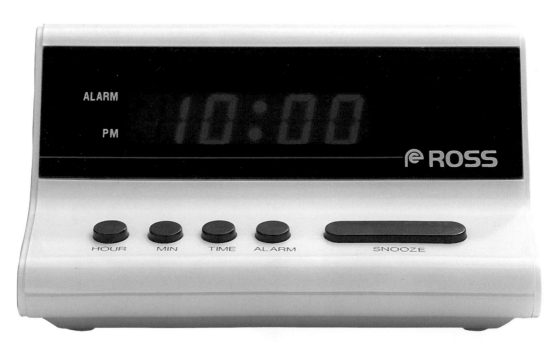

10 o'clock.

What time is it?

To do:
Write these times down
as digital time.

21

We measure time in hours, days, weeks, months and years.

24 hours = 1 day. 7 days = 1 week.
52 weeks = 1 year. 12 months = 1 year.

6 years old today.

How old will this girl be
in 12 months time?

To do:
When is your birthday?
How many months old
are you?

answers

Page 5   Tower number 2 is tallest
Page 7   The green pencil is longest. The red pencil
          is shortest
Page 9   5 boxes tall
Page 11   8cm long. 6cm wide
Page 13   The wash bag is lighter
Page 15   The flour weighs 500 grams or half a
          kilogram.
          To do: The sugar weigh 500g more than
          the biscuits
Page 19   1 clock shows 5 o'clock. The others show
          2 o'clock.
          To do: 4 o'clock, 9 o'clock, 12 o'clock
Page 21   10 o'clock. **To do:** 8:00, 10:00, 4.50
Page 23   7 years old

index